Nathan Wright

Memorial Address

Delivered Before the Second Presbyterian church and society of

Cincinnati, Sunday evening, April 28, 1872

Nathan Wright

Memorial Address
Delivered Before the Second Presbyterian church and society of Cincinnati, Sunday evening, April 28, 1872

ISBN/EAN: 9783337125714

Printed in Europe, USA, Canada, Australia, Japan

Cover: Foto ©Lupo / pixelio.de

More available books at **www.hansebooks.com**

MEMORIAL ADDRESS

DELIVERED BEFORE THE

SECOND PRESBYTERIAN CHURCH

AND SOCIETY OF CINCINNATI.

SUNDAY EVENING, APRIL 28, 1872.

By NATHANIEL WRIGHT.

Printed by the Session.

CINCINNATI:
ROBERT CLARKE & CO.
1873.

The Church edifice of " THE SECOND PRESBYTERIAN CHURCH AND SOCIETY OF CINCINNATI," *on Fourth Street, having been sold, the purchaser to take possession on the first of May, the last Religious Services of the Society in the Church were held on Sunday evening, April* 28, 1872. *The services commenced with the usual exercises of the day, singing, and prayer by the Pastor, followed by a Memorial Address, by* NATHANIEL WRIGHT, *Senior Elder of the Church.*

ADDRESS.

IT is useful in human life occasionally to pause and review the past. Experience is a wise teacher. Not only the difficulties and successes, the mistakes and the achievements of *ourselves*, but also of those who have gone before us, are lessons to be studied for our own good. Now and then some crisis in affairs, some transition from old scenes to new, seem to call upon us especially for such review. The benefits of it are not merely the instruction it may impart. But more than this, it serves to keep alive in our hearts our sympathy with our Fathers—with those who have gone before us—to bind together the past and the present generations in bonds of perpetual love.

We are about to leave this house in which we have worshiped so long, and to occupy another. To many of us the associations of the place are touching and strong—to all of us they are interesting. Here, for forty-two years, from week to week, we have listened to the truths of God, seeking to train us for duty and for heaven; here, from time to time, we have met our Redeemer at his board, to quicken our remembrance of him and our love; here, some of us have first felt the love of Jesus and professed his name before men ; here, our children have been baptized and grown up with us in the worship of the Most High ; here, in the Sunday-schools so many have been trained in the paths of piety ; here, we have so often met the kind, familiar faces of each other, and felt the powerful sympathy of social devotion. But all material things of earth must pass away. Their uses are temporary, and we must learn to part with them cheerfully. "Set not your affections on them," says the apostle.

But the *associations* of the place and its history are not to be parted with. They are to be cherished as a part of the life of the church, to be carried with it to its new abode and be remembered perpetually. It has, therefore, been thought proper, that, before leaving the house, we should spend an hour together in reviewing its past; that when we bid farewell to the building, we may take with us all the influences for good associated with it. The speaker has been selected for this service by reason of his long connection with the society, and he begs your indulgence and your patience; for I do not feel like attempting a formal, dignified address— rhetorical display "plays round the head, but comes not to the heart." I would speak to you, my brethren and friends, in the free, familiar way of a brother in a family circle. I would aid you in keeping in memory the incidents, the persons, the labors, the feelings of the church and the dealings of God with us ; in a word, all those associations which constitute the personal identity of a church, which make it seem the same after all its members have changed.

There is an incident in the history of the Hebrews which illustrates this idea, and shows the power of these memories of the past. The Israelites had been released from centuries of bondage in Egypt, had spent forty years of wandering life in the wilderness, had reached the banks of the Jordan, across which lay their permanent home—the home in which they and their children, from generation to generation, were to be trained in the service of God.

At this juncture, Moses, the man of God, that great and good man, the noblest character in all human history—who can think of him without excitement—

> " This was the truest warrior
> That ever buckled sword ;
> This the most gifted poet
> That ever breathed a word ;
> And never earth's philosopher
> Traced, with his golden pen,
> On the deathless page, truths half so sage
> As he wrote down for men."

Moses, I say, makes to the nation his parting address. *He* was not allowed to pass over the Jordan. God had appointed his unknown grave in a vale among the mountains of Moab. This address is the book of Deuteronomy, strictly a memorial address, recalling to mind the events of their past history and the dealings of God with them—so touching in sympathy for the people he had led so long and loved so well, though

they had grieved him so sorely. These memories of
the past, so woven into the hearts of that people, have
preserved their national identity for more than three
thousand years.

To refer to such wonderful history in illustration of
the humble affairs of one little church, may seem osten-
tatious. But is it really so? Is not the mission of the
Christian church a higher and a nobler service than even
that of the Jews? *Their* mission was to keep alive
upon earth the knowledge of the true God; but it was
confined to their own nation. *Ours* is, to spread the
light of the glorious gospel of the Son of God over all
the world. *Their* history, with its awful demonstrations
of Almighty power, its earthquakes, and thunders, and
pestilence, was terrible to the human senses. *Ours* is
the quiet and gentle influence of kindness and love—
the silent dew, the mild sunshine, so blessing all the
earth—a power surpassing all other among men, for it
comes down from heaven and God is Love. "Not by
might nor by power, but by my spirit, saith the Lord."
Surely such service is worthy all our efforts. It is in
this service, like the Jews of old, that we cherish these
memories of the past among ourselves.

I propose to speak first of the secular affairs of the
society; then of the church proper and its doings, its
members and their social influences.

The first records of the society are January 29, 1816,
though its organization was not authoritatively settled
till 1817. It originated virtually in a small colony
from the first Presbyterian Church of the city. If there

was anything of the workings of imperfect human nature on either side in that origin, it was no marvel upon earth. They were pious and devoted people. If we can esteem and love only those who are perfect, where in this world shall we find anybody to love? Nay, where shall we find anybody to love us?

They began few in number and a feeble society. They worshiped for some two years in such rooms as they could find about the city, in private houses, in school-rooms and the like. In an application to the Presbytery for a minister to supply them, they offer the sum of $550 per annum. In 1817 or 1818 they erected a small frame building on the east side of Walnut street, a little north of Fifth, where they continued to worship for about twelve years. The erection of this humble building cost them not a little of trouble and anxiety. One of those mothers in Israel used to relate that at one time they were stopped in the work for want of lumber; they had not been able to lay it in beforehand, and there was none in the city, and none expected.

They had a prayer-meeting at her house, and, among other things, prayed earnestly that God would help them along with the work. Next morning some of the members happening to be at the river, saw a raft of lumber afloat which the men aboard could not land for want of help. So they hurried out, helped them ashore, and in return got a supply of lumber very cheap, and thanked God for it. The architect of the court-house had a lot of window-sash, which, through some mistake,

would not fit, and gave them to the church at half price.
Thus it was that little church was built.

The salary of Mr. Root, the first settled pastor, was
nominally one thousand dollars; but it was fixed at a
time when the circulating medium here was greatly de-
preciated, and ultimately contracts of that period were
generally settled at one-third discount for specie; so
that Mr. Root received only six hundred and sixty-six
dollars in coin. I presume his salary was ultimately
raised above that sum, though I find no record of it.

In 1827 the subject of building a new church was
agitated, and meetings held on the subject. A committee was appointed to solicit subscriptions, and after
one or two failures, a plan of subscription was adopted,
giving to the subscribers the control in building the
church. Under this plan about one-third of the ulti-
mate cost was raised, and it was decided to go on with
the work, trusting to Providence for the rest. The
location was a matter of much discussion. Different
sites were talked of, somewhat out of the way, costing
some two thousand dollars more or less. But there was
among us a presentiment that the church was to become
a distinguished one, and perhaps a little of worldly am-
bition to make it so. This spot was selected as peculiarly eligible; central, conspicuous, yet retired and
quiet. There were then scarcely any buildings on the
square, and no business on Fourth street. In the
spring of 1828, a contract of purchase was made with
the Bank of the United States for five thousand dollars.

The subscribers appointed a building committee, to whom was intrusted the entire and exclusive care of erecting the building, and doing everything relating thereto. The society, as such, did not interfere in the matter. The design in selecting this committee was to include in it all those leading business men of the society, who felt a special interest in it and were willing to devote their time to the object, and their means, so far as they were able. Thus it was in fact the substance of the society for pecuniary purposes.

This committee were Jacob Burnet, Martin Baum, John H. Groesbeck, Timothy S. Goodman, Jonathan Bates, John T. Drake, Henry Starr, and Nathaniel Wright.

The first three, Burnet, Baum, and Groesbeck, were the leading members, pillars of strength wherever they stood. Judge Burnet is known to all who know the history of our state or the nation. Probably no other man has exerted so great influence in the judicial and legislative affairs of the state. He was a *good*, as well as a great man. He was not a member of the church; but those who knew him intimately, knew him to be an earnest follower of the Redeemer, and that he had some peculiar technical reasons for not uniting with the church.

Martin Baum was a distinguished merchant of the earliest period of the city, proverbial for unostentatious honesty. The German emigrants over the country were in the habit of requiring him to keep their money for them. He was of cultivated taste in architecture, and procured from Maryland the distinguished architect who planned and superintended the building.

John H. Groesbeck was long a model merchant and banker; one who did so much to maintain a high tone of mercantile integrity in the city. He was one of the kindest and best men that ever lived.

Among the junior members of the committee, Timothy S. Goodman was probably the oldest; a man of modest and retiring disposition, highly esteemed by all, long a successful merchant and banker, though finally overtaken by adversity.

Jonathan Bates and John T. Drake also were merchants, men of sterling worth and highly respected.

Henry Starr was a lawyer of distinguished talents and learning—distinguished by the epithet, an honest lawyer—distinguished also by the out-spoken frankness—abruptness even—with which he would condemn or check anything which he disapproved. One Sunday during service here, the organ continued to play, after the minister had risen in the pulpit to proceed, the organist being a new hand or inattentive. Mr. Starr started up in that aisle, and called out in a voice which made the house ring, " Stop that noise !"

Of the remaining member of the committee, I have nothing to say, for you see he is yet alive : all the others are gone, though the widows of three of them still remain : Mrs. Goodman, Mrs. Drake (now Mrs. Strong), and Mrs. Bates, President of the Orphan Asylum ; all honored and blessed in the decline of life.

This committee had a laborious and difficult task in

building the church. They took hold of it and managed it as a work of their own, expecting to be personally responsible for the expense incurred. Ultimately some of them doubled their subscriptions; they borrowed money on their individual responsibility; advanced money in various ways; and finally several who had thus become large creditors, received pews in payment of their claims. The whole cost was about $30,000. We had much difficulty in raising the money. With such men engaged, some of whom have since ranked as men of large wealth, you can hardly realize this difficulty. But we must look back to those times, and financial matters as they then were. The city had passed through a most remarkable and instructive experience. The war, which attracted so much attention to the west, closed about the beginning of 1815. For three or four years after that, emigration was flowing in torrents into all this region, creating great demand for real estate. Everybody was excited with the universal prosperity. All were investing their money in lands. Near the close of 1818, the reverse and the revulsion came. All the local banks, which furnished the entire circulating medium here, suspended payment and finally wound up their affairs. For three or four years we struggled on with their largely depreciated notes, for there was no other money. The Branch of the United States Bank for awhile received them, but finally demanded specie or its equivalent. That was not to be had, and in the fall of 1820, its current paper was nearly all protested, some million and a half in amount, and judgments generally recovered therefor in the United States court, in 1822. The old business men were generally broken up. Those who had real estate seemed the worst off, for they could hardly pay their taxes. Nobody would buy lands at any price, for the public had become thoroughly sick of them. Men whose real estate has since been counted by millions, considered themselves insolvent.

In 1824, affairs began slowly to improve, but up to the time of building the church, lands generally were a drug in market, in no way available as money to the owners. The junior members of our committee were mostly young in business and of limited means. You will see, therefore, that for us the work we had undertaken was no trifle. In ready cash we were all poor.

There is a lesson here which should not be forgotten. Some of the debts hung over us like a dead weight for a long time; and a *dead weight* they truly were, as any man will realize who can't pay his honest debts. The last of four payments for the ground fell due May 1, 1831; one installment only had been paid. The bank afterward got judgment in ejectment and might have turned us out of the house at any moment. Finally, about ten years after the purchase, in January, 1838, the matter was settled by taking a deed and giving a note and mortgage for the balance due, $4,367, payable in July of that year. Even this note laid over and judgment was recovered on it, and the church advertised for sale on execution years afterward. We were not worse than other people; but we did not realize till it was too late, the discredit to the cause and the disadvantage to the church of debts hanging over it.

The labors of the committee in detail will be of little interest. Mr. Walters, the architect, superintended all the details of the work, and that with such integrity and skill as resulted in great economy. There were no lumping contracts. The committee met regularly twice a week for some time, and afterward once, spending an afternoon or evening discussing matters, sometimes sorely perplexed how to raise funds to keep on with the work. There never was the least dissension among us. If we differed in opinion, we discussed the subject candidly till we agreed.

The corner-stone was laid May 13, 1829, in presence of a large congregation, with appropriate solemnities. Mr. Root delivered an impressive address. In the corner-stone, the northeast corner, were deposited various mementos of the time; among others, the names of the officers of the church and society, of various public officers, of the Governor of the State, Allen Trimble, the newspapers of the day, the population of the city (22,000), the closing paragraph of the Pastor's address on the occasion, which was as follows: "To God, who loveth the gates of Zion more than the dwellings of Jacob, we commit the interests of this rising Temple. May it bless a hundred generations. Here may converts be multiplied as drops of the morning dew, and an immense number be qualified for heaven. May its walls be called salvation and its gates praise. May it stand a beacon to invite the stranger and the heavy laden sinner to recline under its shadow and to receive its consolations, until the last shock of time shall demolish the stablest works of man, and the general conflagration of the world wind up the arcana of nature."

During the ensuing year the building was completed, and on the 20th of May, 1830, was publicly dedicated to the worship of the Triune God.   The Pastor, in his address on that occasion, says, " My brethren, ye have built a house of prayer unto the Lord. Be not high-minded, but fear, lest ye be likened unto those who 'built the tombs of the prophets, and garnished the sepulchres of the righteous.'   Though this building is honorable to this growing city, and confers deserved commendation upon those who have reared it, and commodiously adapted to the purposes of worship, it is not necessarily the gate of heaven.   It is possible for you to perish from the inner courts of the sanctuary, and from the very horns of the altar."

The building was regarded as an ornament to the young city—was commended by the press as a work of art, a specimen of a chaste style of architecture, a Grecian chapel with a Doric portico, a style which has stood the criticism of two thousand years; and it does, in fact, compare favorably with the gaudy and costly style of churches, which has since become fashionable.

The society was incorporated by act of the legislature of February 11, 1829.

The first board of trustees under the charter was elected May 4, 1829, and were Jacob Burnet, Martin Baum, John H. Groesbeck, Nathaniel Wright, Timothy S. Goodman, Jesse Kimball, and John T. Drake. The next year Henry Starr and William W. Green, (son of one of the original members of the church,) were elected in place of Kimball, and Drake, the latter having died the winter preceding. Soon after, Jonathan Bates came into the board and a majority of these were generally re-elected, from year to year, for ten or twelve years, and some for twenty years or more.

The city had a large clock, with no place to put it, and in January, 1831, the use of the tower and the bell was granted them for it, and there it still remains.

In 1837, the organ was put up, having been constructed for the society in Cambridge, Massachusetts, under the care of Timothy B. Mason, at a cost of three thousand dollars, besides incidentals, which was paid by private subscriptions.

Thus the work was finished, as you see it now, except the colored glass and the two south windows closed, matters done long after, under the name of improvements. Since then we have progressed, in secular affairs, in the common-place routine of like societies, with some difficulties and embarrassments; but we have paid off all our debts and been generally prosperous.

I come now to speak of the church proper, the life and soul of all this secular labor. True, the church has its secular cares and troubles; for it works among men and is managed by them; but the essence of it is, the spiritual and the heavenly.

In speaking of Christians and their doings, we can not be too often reminded, that they are but human beings; of course frail and fallible, liable to mistakes and misjudgments, earnest in their feelings in proportion to the importance of the cause. *We*, frail as they, are not to sit in judgment on them. "Judge not, that ye be not judged." There may be more than a mote in *our own* eyes, when we attempt to pick one out of *theirs*. Yet it is not improper, in giving the history of good men, to refer to their faults as well as their virtues. The faults of our Lord's disciples are fully and freely told, and so of all the best characters in the Bible.

During the year 1814 or 1815, some members of the first church, with others, applied to Presbytery for the organization of a second church, which was not granted; and from the action of Presbytery some of the parties took the matter to Synod. The Synod directed the Presbytery to consider the matter, indicating that, if they found a sufficient number of suitable persons desiring it, such church should be established. Pursuant to this direction, a special meeting of Presbytery was called for January 3, 1816. This meeting was a long, arduous, and excited one, and a real curiosity in church history. Adjourning from the 6th to the 17th of the month, they occupied seven days exclusively on this subject. Only three members, one being an elder, acted and voted in the opposition, but *they* were earnest and persevering, and skillful in parliamentary tactics. A multitude of questions, dilatory or otherwise, were raised and disposed of, and at last, on the 19th of January, Presbytery reached a final vote on the merits.

By that vote they established the Second Presbyterian Church, directing its records to commence from that date, and appointed the Rev. James Kemper to preach for them. From this decision appeal was taken to Synod.

At the session of Presbytery, in Dayton, April 2, 1816, the matter was brought up again, and that body, by a majority of one—two members not voting—voted to reconsider the proceedings of January 19th, and passed an order restraining the members from acting as a church, and agreed to hold a meeting at Lebanon, June 25th, to consider the whole matter. At Lebanon, the Presbytery, after discussion, referred the whole subject to Synod. Thus the whole matter on both sides was before that body; and in October, 1816, the Synod set aside the proceedings at Dayton as irregular, and confirmed the original action of Presbytery, establishing the church. From this decision an appeal was taken to the General Assembly. At the meeting of that body in May, 1817, this appeal was taken up, and after some discussion the appeal was withdrawn by the appellants. This was the final end of the controversy. The effect of it was to leave the order of January 19th, establishing the church, in full force.

During the pendency of this litigation, the church seems to have been in doubt as to what they were authorized to do in the way of organization, and appointed four members, by the name of trustees, with authority to attend to the admission of members, and under their supervision several were admitted.

On the 29th of January, ten days after the original order of the Presbytery establishing the church, is their first meeting appearing of record. The members were eleven in number, viz: Robert Wallace and his wife Rebecca, Edith Wallace, Mrs. Burnet, Mrs. Baum, Mrs. Green, Jane Fleming, Daniel Tremper, Henrietta Tremper, Dan Davis, and Sarah Spinning. For some time the numbers of the church increased slowly. When Mr. Root came, three or four years after, the number present was only thirty-one. During his ministry, 344 were added.

The organization of the church being authoritatively settled, they proceeded, on the 10th of July, 1817, to elect ruling elders, and Robert Wallace, Daniel Tremper, John Kelso, and Jesse Churchill were chosen. Of the patriarch, Robert Wallace, I shall have occasion to speak hereafter. Jesse Churchill was an interesting old man. He had led a seafaring life, and had his full share of wild adventures by sea and by land. Finally his health had failed him, and he had come here to end his days in quiet, with children who had settled here. He was a humble, devoted Christian. One of his sons in some way had occasioned him grief, and he used to say, "Ah! children, when they are little, tread on our knees; but when they are old, they tread on our hearts." Some here may remember him when we first came into this house, seated there in the aisle, in an easy chair, which kind women of the church had provided for him. His death was remarkable. He retired at night in usual health, though feeble; in the morning, not appearing at his usual time, they went to his bed and found him apparently in quiet sleep, but he was dead.

Of subsequent elders not now living, there are several known to you personally or by reputation : John Rice, elected July, 1821; James McIntyre, elected August, 1824; Dr. James Warren, and John H. Groesbeck, elected September, 1828; Augustus Moore, elected March, 1832; Dr. Thomas D. Mitchell, afterward medical professor in the University at Lexington, Ky., elected January, 1834; Henry Starr, and Isaac G. Burnet, so long mayor of the city and judge of the first city court, elected December, 1834; Dr. Reuben D. Mussey, professor in the Ohio Medical College, and so distinguished in his profession; Ebenezer S. Padgett and John C. Macy, elected March, 1840. All men of great worth and usefulness.

It was some time before a pastor was settled. For a considerable time Rev. Samuel Robinson supplied the pulpit—a man of learning and talents, but we are compelled to remember his latter years with sadness. Rev. William Arthur, a good old man, afterward supplied the pulpit, and also the Rev. John Thomson, father of the distinguished missionary and author, who has spent a life of great usefulness in Palestine.

Rev. David Root was elected pastor, September 4, 1819, but did not commence his services till the latter part of 1820. He continued pastor till the spring of 1832, when he resigned. During his pastorate this house was erected, and the church and congregation had largely increased, and taken a leading rank in the Christian world.

Rev. Lyman Beecher had been appointed professor in Lane Seminary, and came here to discharge the duties of that office, and of President of the Faculty, in November, 1832. From that time he supplied the pulpit, and was formally elected pastor, March 11, 1833, and so continued to the fall of 1843, when he resigned. His high reputation for talents and piety is matter of general history. He was a man of brilliant intellect, of untiring zeal in the cause, and of great usefulness. He was original and somewhat peculiar, both in manner and thought. In preaching, his most striking passages seemed the inspiration of the moment—when he raised his spectacles to his forehead, and his sparkling eyes to the audience, and something came forth which struck us like electricity. He was deeply reverential at heart, though sometimes his strong, abrupt language seemed almost to belie it : as on one occasion I remember he said in prayer, "O Lord, keep us from despising our rulers, and keep them from acting so that we ca n't help it."

It was during his pastorate that the Old and New School controversy came to its crisis by separation. It existed previously, and in sympathy with our pastor, Mr. Root, without any formal action, we had drifted into the New School party. Indeed, the controversy seems not to have been one belonging to common people, but rather one of theological science ; and if a layman may be allowed to say it, savored somewhat of the speculations of human reason on matters above human ken. Dr. Beecher went through a long trial for heresy in this house. But the sooner these things are forgotten the better. No doubt many who wrangled on earth are rejoicing together in heaven. Charity is the chief jewel in Christian character.

Under Dr. Beecher a special effort was made to cherish congregational singing. A church singing-school, including very young children, met every week, and gave occasional concerts. The theory was, that almost every child may learn to sing, if he begins early enough ; and that the power of this exhilarating branch of worship would be largely increased by the congregation at large uniting in it, as is illustrated anywhere by the effect of a popular song in a crowd.

In the spring of 1843, a colony of 36 was dismissed from this church for the purpose of organizing the George Street Presbyterian Church, since known as the Seventh Street Church.

The whole number admitted to the church during Dr. Beecher's pastorate was 540, of whom 240 were on profession.

The Rev. John P. Cleveland was elected pastor August 2, 1843, and commenced his services near the close of that year, and resigned the charge in December, 1845. During his brief pastorate 57 were admitted to the church, of whom six were on profession. He was a man of fluent eloquence and commanding manner.

The Rev. Samuel W. Fisher was elected pastor, October 26, 1846; commenced his services in April,

1847, and resigned in July, 1858, to assume the duties of President of Hamilton College, in the State of New York, to which he had been elected. He was a man greatly beloved and esteemed, of a gentle but earnest nature, and of a cultivated, classic taste. His many published sermons show his ability in that department of service; but his health was broken down at last by overburden of mental efforts, and he was compelled to withdraw from all public labors.

Overtaxing the mental powers! We ought to realize more than we do, this terrible evil, which is prostrating so many of the clergymen of the present age. One after another of the ablest and best of men, struck down in the prime and vigor of life, and sent to their graves, or left to drag out a feeble and useless existence!

The simple toil of leading the humble soul to the Saviour is not exhausting, but the educated and cultivated are not satisfied with this. To attract them requires intellectual skill and power, and all classes must be approached with worldly wisdom. Hence this havoc among the clergy in our large cities. No other service among men requires such intense and incessant intellectual effort.

Among the apostles, Paul only occupied this field of exhausting labor. Observe how God provided him with rest and recreation. A large part of his life was spent in traveling. For two whole years he lay a quiet prisoner in Palestine, and, for a considerable time afterward, in Rome also. If we must have the intellectual power and labors of Paul, we must treat our clergy as God treated him.

During Dr. Fisher's pastorate, 426 members were added to the church, of whom 178 were on profession.

The Rev. M. L. P. Thompson was elected pastor, December 15, 1859; commenced his services in the following March, and resigned in May, 1865. During his pastorate, 229 were added to the church, of whom 106 were on profession.*

The Rev. James L. Robertson was elected pastor, April 3, 1867; commenced his services in May following, and resigned about the beginning of November, 1870. During his pastorate 127 were added to the church, of whom 62 were on profession. He was a young man of great promise, of earnest and active piety, of the kindest social affections and manners, and greatly beloved by all. He accepted a call to a commanding church in Rochester, New York, which was peculiarly attractive and promising to him, inasmuch as it restored him to the vicinity of a large circle of old friends and acquaintances.

The Rev. Thomas H. Skinner, D. D., our present pastor, was elected July 12, 1871, and entered on his services about the beginning of November of that year —sent to us, we feel assured, as a special blessing from the Lord of the vineyard. If he does not prove so, it will be our fault, not his.

I will now speak briefly of some general labors of

---

* In consequence of what has transpired since the address was delivered, a paragraph here is stricken out.

the church itself, and its members. The whole number added to the church from its commencement to April 1, 1872, as nearly accurate as I can state it, is 1,876, of which 847 were on profession. The numbers of the congregation have never been large, for the size of the house would not permit it. There have been several interesting seasons of revival, in which considerable numbers of converts were received into the church, one of the most interesting of which was in the spring of 1843, under Dr. Beecher. But the largest part of those so received have been in small numbers from time to time, scattered over the whole period, indicating a continuous religious interest.

The church and society has regularly contributed, from year to year, to the various benevolent and religious enterprises of the time. The total amount of these contributions, I have not been able to ascertain. For ten years, ending April 1, 1857, under Dr. Fisher, they amounted to $70,600. For ten years, ending April 1, 1871, they were $70,090. These are exclusive of the expenses of the church for itself, its own Sunday-school and poor, which, for six years, ending April 1, 1871, averaged a little over $9,000 per annum.

In several religious enterprises, of great usefulness, some of our members have been especially active and efficient. The Young Men's Bible Society originated in our church, though not confined to it in its organization, and owes much of its success to some of our members. The Young Men's Christian Union, also, has derived much of its energy and zeal from our members. In the Bethel cause, also, which has been so widely and so nobly sustained, our members have contributed their share, both of service and money. That noble institution, the Orphan Asylum, owes a large share of its success and good management to the energy and devotion of our women. To the Lane Seminary and its students, we have given frequent aid.

The Children's Home has been liberally aided by some of our members. Without ostentation, it has been largely efficient in taking care of, and providing for destitute children. It occupies the house on Third street, west of Elm, long known as the residence of George Williamson.

The Young Women's Christian Association, in its quiet way, has exerted a blessed influence, and our young women have been very active in it.

The Sewing Society of the church, unpretending and almost unknown, has sent comforts to many naked and destitute.

The Ladies' City Missionary Society, of our church, with silent, persevering industry, has long been sending the sound of the Gospel into obscure and forsaken places, and to ears that otherwise would not have heard it. Who does not know and revere that good man, Horace Bushnell, now old and infirm, so meek, so faithful, and so wise in the service of his Master!

The Young Men's Home Missionary Society, originally of this church, has been of great and extensive usefulness. It was organized in 1848, during Dr. Fisher's pastorate, with Wm. H. Neff for its first president, for the immediate purpose of sustaining a missionary in Iowa. Supporting him till he no longer needed their aid, they engaged in various missionary labors in the city, employing in the service young men preparing for the ministry, and directing special attention to organizing Sabbath-schools. The first they established was at the corner of Eighth street and Central Avenue, under the superintendence of William H. Neff, and was highly successful. The second, on Fourth street, between Wood and Stone, under the superintendence of O. N. Bush, and was specially useful. The third, near the base of Mount Auburn, afterward removed to Race, near Thirteenth street. The fourth, on Poplar street near Freeman, under the superintendence of L. H. Sargent and H. B. Olmstead, which finally resulted in establishing the flourishing church and erecting the fine building there, so long under the care of the Rev. Joseph Chester. The fifth, on Sixth street, west of Freeman, under the care of Col. S. S. Fisher and L. R. Hull, afterward permanently located on Carr street, near Sixth, and the second school incorporated with it. It is large and flourishing, has been provided with weekly preaching, and very probably may result in the organization of a church. Within a few weeks past, it has been transferred to the care of the Third Presbyterian Church. It is known as the Olivet Mission School.

The minor labors of this society are various, for they have been very enterprising. Their contributions have

amounted to $7,000 in a year, and the number of
scholars in their schools to 1,500.

The most important of all these enterprises are the
Sunday-schools. Their great object is, to preoccupy
the infant mind with the knowledge and the love of
God; to surround it with associations of piety and rec-
titude, before it has become contaminated and hardened
by a wicked world. True, they can not supply the
duty which God has so specially assigned to parents.
But where parents fail, they can, in some degree, supply the defect; and they ever aid parents by the atmos-
phere of piety, which they throw around the children.
There is no estimating the numbers which have been
led to heaven through this instrumentality.

Our own Sunday-school commenced in the earliest
period of the church. It was then chiefly the work of
women. Dr. Waldo, one of its early superintendents,
made its first report to the Sunday School Union, in 1827.
Its number was then about 300, meeting part of the
time in the old church, and part of the time in the old
Lancaster Seminary, where the Cincinnati College now
stands. From that time to this, the school has flour-
ished and been greatly blessed. It has been well supplied with a library, and several of our young men
have devoted themselves to it as superintendents. The
young women have been specially earnest and successful as teachers, and the influence of woman, the old
and the young, has been felt through all its history,
breathing into it a spirit of life and love, concentrating

upon it the social sympathies of the church. Many from this school have been added to the church.

In February, 1870, another Sabbath-school was organized in the church, to be held in the afternoon, for the purpose of gathering in children who did not attend the morning school. Its numbers have steadily increased; it is now largely attended and highly prosperous.

The German Mission Sabbath-school was established by our mem bersin 1846, Elder E. S. Padgett, Wm. H. Mussey, and Peter Rudolph Neff, being successively the first superintendents. It was first located at the corner of Thirteenth and Walnut streets, was several times removed, and obtained its largest growth (400 in number), at the northeast corner of Ninth and Walnut streets, under Mr. Neff, a second time superintendent. It is now located on Race street, above Fourteenth, and is flourishing.

A school for the Germans was also established in the northwest part of the city, under the care of the Rev. Mr. Winness, under whose devoted labors, and the aid of our society, the school ripened into a church with a church edifice, and that church, into a second one with like accommodations, doing much good among that class of our population.

The Pilgrim Mission School, in the eastern part of the city, corner of Fifth and Lock streets, was established by some of our members some twenty-five years since, and has been sustained and successfully managed by them. It ultimately resulted in a church organized there

by the same name, which has recently united with the
Broadway church.

I have already mentioned the five schools established
by our Young Men's Home Missionary Society. All
together they have amounted to a very extensive and
very useful Sunday-school influence.

I have been able only to refer very briefly to our
local, religious, and benevolent enterprises. It would
require volumes to do full justice to them all. Including the national associations, we have contributed
habitually to about twenty such organizations, besides
various other occasioned contributions.

We can not do justice to the history of our church,
perhaps not of any church, without referring specially
to the influence of woman. It is a power so great in
its silent workings, that we need to study it well in our
plans for usefulness. And yet it is a critical topic for
a public speaker, perhaps a dangerous one, for he may
bring upon himself the frowns of the most worthy of
the sex, by seeming to trifle with the retiring delicacy
of their nature. But I will beg pardon in advance, de-
claring that if I should seem rude, I do not intend it.

We can not read any history profitably without re-
cognizing the power of woman for evil as well as for
good. What a sad thing for us all was the failure of
our mother Eve in the garden of Eden! In Jewish
history, Jezebel, Queen of Israel, daughter of a pagan
king and a worshiper of Baal, married her daughter to
a king of Judah, and through her introduced pagan worship into Jerusalem, the traces of which continued there

till the time of the captivity, three hundred years after. Her husband, Ahab, had threatened the life of Elijah; but the prophet sought him and met him face to face. But when Jezebel made the same threat, he fled for his life to the wilderness. The spite of a woman cost John the Baptist his head; on the other hand, the love and the quick faith of woman were the great comfort of our Saviour upon earth. When he appeared to the disciples the evening after the resurrection, he could hardly persuade them it was himself. He had to show them his pierced hands and feet, to eat with them, and talk a long time with them, before they began to realize it. But when, on the morning of the same day, Mary Magdalen met him in the garden, at first taking him for a stranger, the single word "Mary," spoken in his familiar voice, carried entire conviction to her quiet womanly heart, and she rushes up to him, crying out, "Rabboni," as much as to say, "my dear Lord."

It is in connection with the church, especially, that the power of woman for good is so great. The foundation of that power is love, the great attribute of Deity; that Divine love, which Christ came down from heaven to manifest. With that kind and gentle nature which God has given her, she melts hearts which are ice to all others. At home among the little ones, in the social circles of life, even in the contests and collisions of the world, that mild loving spirit is a power like that of angels—silent and unseen it may be, but it prevails when all other forces fail. It conquers by yielding.

What woman does not know that she can rule a man, if she will take care not to let him know it.

Some modern reformers seem to think that the power of woman would be increased by giving her the ballot. Alas for the day when her gentle nature shall be thus involved in the coarse wranglings of party politics !—a work which would harden the heart of an angel, if he would meddle with it. It would leave her but a Sampson shorn of his locks.

Of the first eleven members of this church, eight were women. Tradition ascribes to them the principal agency in the various plans for religious culture. They were the life of the first Sunday-school, four or five of them attended every Sunday to teach and direct; they collected the schools, provided the funds, and procured superintendents. From that day to this, woman's influence has been the life and the joy of the school. So many young women as teachers—those birds of Paradise, with their little flocks around them, training them to remember and to love their Creator and their Redeemer; to be kind to each other and do right. With what joy will these scenes be recalled in future life! With what exceeding joy be remembered in heaven !

The Orphan Asylum, the Ladies' City Missionary Society, the Young Women's Christian Association, the Sewing Society, the Children's Home, are charities especially dispensed by women, and their great usefulness is well known. What multitudes have been rescued from ruin, or relieved from distress by these labors! In many other benevolent enterprises, her aid has been an essential element.

But it is not in these public charities, important as they are, that the great strength of female influence lies. It lies in that silent, unseen power, to be imagined but not described, which God has given to woman's love over the human soul. The infant in his cradle feels it, the first of his emotions; the child as he grows up feels it, stronger than his wayward propensities; the youth, among the temptations of vice, feels it, and is restrained; the young man, as he begins to look out on the path of life before him, feels it, overpowering all other emotions; the passionate man, enraged by angry collisions, feels it, and becomes gentle; the old man, worn down by trouble and sorrow, feels it, and is comforted; even the hardened old reprobate, on his way to the gallows, feels it, remembering his mother, and sheds tears.

Such is woman's power, and with the guidance and aid of the church, it is immense for good. In training the young, in all her social relations, in all the sweet charities of life, its silent influences are felt—*silent* as the falling dew; for these labors are not to be numbered or proclaimed—are hardly known to themselves even, the left hand not knowing what the right hand doeth. Yet we should learn to appreciate them, that we may never attempt to divert woman from her appropriate sphere.

In this connection, I can hardly avoid referring to something of family history in the church, to show how these influences have operated. I have been personally

acquainted, more or less, with five successive generations. I have seen how the seed planted by the first of
them has grown and spread its branches far and wide,
and more or less of the same fruit is found upon all.
Of several examples, I will mention the one most remarkable for the numbers involved.

The patriarch, Robert Wallace, was one of the original members of the church, himself and wife and four
daughters, being six of the first eleven members. He
was one of the first four elders. His other children
were Mrs. Wade and Mrs. Perry ; Rev. Matthew G.
Wallace, at an early day pastor of the first church; Robert Wallace, Jr., and David C. Wallace, the last unmar-
ried.

Six families of these are well known among us. The
name of Wallace is blended with that of Burnet, Baum,
Green, Wade, Groesbeck, Neff, Shillito, McLean, and
many others at a later day ; and the numerous descendants are found in Cincinnati, Chicago, St. Louis, New
York, London, and other places in the interior.

Mrs. Burnet was a woman of remarkable energy and
devotion in the cause, as well as of the most untiring
assiduity in all the kind charities of life. She was regarded as a kind of foster-mother in the infancy of
the church. In the first Sunday-school she, with her
mother, Mrs. Baum, and Mrs. John H. Groesbeck,
attended every week, and kept the school prospering.
All the sisters were active in the church ; of the broth-
ers, the clergyman was for many years usefully employed
in this city and vicinity, and ultimately permanently

located in the interior of Indiana. The remaining married brother was well known and respected here. He is gone, but his widow survives him, and well is it said of HER, "her children rise up and call her blessed."

Imagine the numerous descendants scattered all over the land, with their various associations of marriage, friendship, and social relations, involving thousands now, and perhaps millions hereafter, and you have some idea of the influence of that one patriarch Christian on his race. As far as we know the descendants, they all indicate, more or less, the effect of Christian training; and we know it is the law of our nature, that such training will mark, if not fix, the character.

"Just as the twig is bent, the tree's inclined."

In conclusion, let us look back upon our history and see what there is to be carried with us in memory, when we leave this house. We began a little, humble flock, but of strong faith in God. We labored long and patiently through embarrassments and difficulties. We have become what the world calls a strong and leading church. We have, in fact, aided largely in the religious and charitable enterprises which have so greatly distinguished the age. I suppose we may say we have done much good. We have been the means of leading many to heaven. How often here have we seen men and women, young and old, come forward and take the vows of God upon them, and consecrate themselves to the service of the Redeemer! True, our pastors have been the principal agents in this blessed work; yet every one of us should feel that we have done something, however little, and that little may result in more than we have any idea of.

How trifling are worldly pursuits compared with this service! Wealth is desirable to provide us the comforts of life, and enable us to be useful in the world. But wealth of itself!—suppose yourself looking back upon it a hundred years hence, what a frivolous gewgaw will it seem! But a million years hence, looking back to earth, with what exceeding joy will you remember your labors for Christ!

All things earthly are passing away. Of the members of the church at the time we came into this house, I find only four still remaining members—John Shillito, Mrs. Mary B. Perry, Mrs. Timothy S. Goodman, and Miss Jennett Twichell, now Mrs. Bliss. There are some others, then active members of the congregation, who have since joined the church. How many of us members now, will be found here forty-two years hence?

To those of us who have long been here, this place of worship awakens many tender recollections. It is endeared by hallowed associations. But it is of earth, and our affections are not to be set upon it. All the good it has done us may be carried with us wherever we may go. If we are faithful and wise, humble and devoted, we trust that God will prosper us hereafter, even more abundantly than He has done heretofore; and give us all, both those who have gone before us and those who shall come after us, a joyful meeting in a better world.

The Pastor then read the following poem, written by Mrs. M. D. ALLEN:

LINES WRITTEN ON LEAVING THE SECOND PRESBYTERIAN CHURCH.

We come to-day, mid smiles and tears,
   A farewell offering now to bring
To Him who through these lengthen'd years
   Hath taught our hearts and lips to sing;

To sing of that dear guiding hand
   Which led Thy children here to raise,
A feeble few, yet faithful band,
   To Thee, this house of prayer and praise.

When Israel out of bondage came,
   Obedient to Thy sovereign will,
The pillar and the cloud became
   A token of Thy presence still.

So we, through many years of love,
   The pillar and the cloud have seen—
That faithful witness from above,
   To teach our souls on Christ to lean.

Here weary hearts have sought that rest,
   That perfect rest that Jesus gives;
And Faith, and Hope, and Mercy blest,
   Have said, Look up, poor soul, and live!

Here youthful hearts have learn'd to know
   And love the gentle Shepherd's voice,
And, following Him " through weal and woe,"
   Have in His kind commands rejoiced.

How many of that honor'd band,
 Whose hearts were warm with holy fire,
Have safely reach'd " the better land,"
 And heard the welcome, " Come up higher ! "

And we, who yet awhile remain
 To bear the burden and the heat,
Would daily seek that strength to gain,
 Which they receive who on Thee wait.

And when our feet shall nearer reach
 That house above, not made with hands,
And, weary with their pilgrim march,
 We tread with joy the heavenly land ;

O be it ours to hear that word,
 That blessed welcome, " Soul, well done !
Enter the kingdom of thy Lord,
 Enjoy thy rest, receive thy crown."

And as we leave this hallowed spot,
 A spot to heart and memory dear,
Be earthly trials all forgot,
 And Christ and Heaven more blest appear.

The services were then closed by prayer and the benediction, and the people, in silent sadness, took final leave of their old church.

APPENDIX.

The following list contains the names of all those who have been elected as Ruling Elders and Deacons in the church, with dates of their election :

ELDERS.

Elected July 10, 1817.

Robert Wallace.   John Kelso.
Daniel Tremper.   Jesse Churchill.

February 11, 1819.

Samuel Lowry.   John Lewis.

July 17, 1821.

John Rice.   John Dillingham.

August 10, 1824.

James McIntyre.

June 26, 1826.

Ralph Webster.   John Sullivan.

September 25, 1828.

Abraham Halsey.   James Warren, M. D.
John H. Groesbeck.

July 14, 1830.

William B. Tappan.   Philip Skinner.
William W. Greene.

March 5, 1832.

Daniel Corwin.   Augustus Moore.

January 30, 1834.

Nathaniel Wright.   Thomas D. Mitchell, M. D.

December 11, 1834.

Henry Starr.   Isaac G. Burnet.

March 5, 1840.

Reuben D. Mussey, M. D.   Osgood Fifield.
James Calhoun.   Ebenezer S. Padgett.
John Dillingham.   John C. Macy.

March 17, 1852.

Henry Y. Slaymaker.   James Taylor, M. D.
Eliab F. Tucker.   Thomas C. Butler, Jr.

November 20, 1860.

William H. Allen.   Elliott H. Pendleton.
Obadiah N. Bush.   Jacob Graff.
Samuel J. Broadwell.   George B. Bradley.

November 13, 1867.

William H. Mussey, M. D.   William Howard Neff,
                      Jacob Burnet, Jr.

DEACONS.

December 5, 1860.

John F. White, M. D.   Simeon B. Williams.

The acting officers of the church, May 1, 1872, are as follows:

THE REV. THOMAS H. SKINNER, D. D., *Pastor.*

RULING ELDERS.

Nathaniel Wright.   Elliot H. Pendleton.
James Taylor, M. D.   Jacob Graff.
Thomas O. Butler.   William H. Mussey, M. D.
William H. Allen.   William Howard Neff.
Samuel J. Broadwell.   Jacob Burnet, Jr., Clerk.

The names of the superintendents of the Sabbath-schools can not be given, as no perfect record of them is found; at present, the superintendent of the morning school is Elliot H. Pendleton; superintendent of the afternoon school, Peter Rudolph Neff.

The Society was incorporated February 11, 1829, with a provision for the election of seven trustees annually, to manage its secular concerns; this election to be held on the first Monday in May of each year, and the following is a list of the names of those elected. As some were many times re-elected, and, to avoid a constant repetition of names, the time, except the last three years, is divided into several periods, and the names of those serving in each period are given together, without specifying the precise date of each election.

TRUSTEES.

Elected from 1829 *to* 1833, *both years included.*

Jacob Burnet.	John T. Drake.
Martin Baum.	Philip Young.
John H. Groesbeck.	Henry Starr.
Nathaniel Wright.	William W. Greene.
Timothy S. Goodman.	Jonathan Bates.
Jesse Kimball.	Jepthah D. Garrard.

James Hall.

From 1834 *to* 1838, *inclusive.*

Timothy S. Goodman.	George W. Neff.
Jepthah D. Garrard.	Charles S. Clarkson.
Jonathan Bates.	Samuel M. Candler.
Henry Starr.	William F. Barnes.
James Hall.	James Tompkins.
Nathaniel Wright.	Amos P. Holden.
Vachel Worthington.	Eliab F. Tucker.
Henry S. Kellogg.	Stephen Schooley.

From 1839 *to* 1843, *inclusive.*

John H. Groesbeck,	C. P. Barnes.
Henry Starr.	Nathaniel Wright.
Timothy S. Goodman.	John C. Macy.
James Tompkins.	Robert W. Burnet.
Hiram K. Wells.	Alexander H. Ewing.
James Calhoun.	O. M. Mitchell.

Henry S. Kellogg.

From 1844 *to* 1848, *inclusive.*

George W. Neff.
Henry S. Kellogg.
Alexander H. Ewing.
Robert W. Burnet.
Henry Starr.
P. Campbell.

Amos P. Holden.
John H. Groesbeck.
E. S. Padgett.
R. D. Mussey, M. D.
Maynard French.

From 1849 *to* 1854, *inclusive.*

John H. Groesbeck.
Henry Starr.
Robert W. Burnet.
Amos P. Holden.
E. S. Padgett.
R. D. Mussey, M. D.

Maynard French.
John Shillito.
N. C. McLean.
Charles Goodman.
E. P. Starr.
William H. Neff.

From 1855 *to* 1859, *inclusive.*

John H. Groesbeck.
Robert W. Burnet.
E. S. Padgett.
Maynard French.
Samuel J. Broadwell.
Maskell E. Curwen.
Frederick G. Huntington.

John Shillito.
E. P. Starr.
William H. Neff.
O. N. Bush.
Jacob Graff.
A. W. Neff.
O. M. Mitchell.

From 1860 *to* 1864, *inclusive.*

John H. Groesbeck.
E. S. Padgett.
Jacob Graff.
Frederick G. Huntington.
M. E. Curwen.
R. W. Burnet.
Eli Johnson.

Elliot H. Pendleton.
William S. Groesbeck.
George Wilshire.
A. S. Winslow.
Pollock Wilson.
Aaron F. Perry.
L. R. Hull.

From 1865 *to* 1869, *inclusive.*

John Shillito.
George Wilshire.
A. S. Winslow.
Hugh McBurney.
Peter Neff.
Samuel J. Hale.

John C. Huntington.
William S. Groesbeck.
L. R. Hull.
R. W. Burnet.
William H. Allen.

[45]

Elected 1870.

John Shillito.
Peter Neff.
Hugh McBurney.

William S. Groesbeck.
George Wilshire.
A. S. Winslow.

John C. Huntington.

Elected 1871.

Hugh McBurney.
Peter Neff.
Thornton M. Hinkle.

Thomas Morrison.
Timothy S. Goodman, Jr.
David B. Lupton.

Henry A. Morrill.

Elected 1872.

John Shillito.
A. S. Winslow.
L. R. Hull.

William H. Harrison.
Thomas Morrison.
Hugh McBurney.

A. W. Williamson.

The last two resigned, and the vacancies supplied by

T. M. Hinkle. Jacob Burnet, Jr.

SALE OF THE CHURCH ON FOURTH STREET—PURCHASE OF A NEW SITE.

In 1864, the question of selling the church lot on Fourth street began to be discussed among the members of the society. That place had become an important business center, and surrounded with the usual disturbances of such a location. There were differences of opinion on the question; some considering it important to the prosperity of the church to have a more quiet and suitable place of worship— while others seemed to cling to this as their old home, and feared that separating from it, would tend to weaken the mutual attachments, as well as the united energy of the members. During 1865 and 1866, the matter was discussed by the society, and plans for improving the old church also considered. In October, 1866, however, the society, at a general meeting, voted to sell, and to purchase another lot and build a new church. But in consequence of the price fixed, and other impediments, matters remained in this situation until 1871. At the annual meeting of the society, May 1, 1871, the trustees were instructed to proceed at once to sell, without restricting them as to price or otherwise, and buy a lot and build a new church. The trustees elected at the same time proceeded in the discharge of this duty. Mr. Robertson, pastor of the church, had resigned the preceding November, and it was thought inexpedient to sell the church until a pastor should be obtained. Dr. Skinner, being elected pastor in July, entered on his services the 1st of November. In November, after much effort to obtain the best terms, the trustees closed a sale of the church to Samuel Fosdick for $160,000, the purchaser to have possession on 1st of May, 1872; the price to be regarded as cash of March 1st, and bearing interest from that date, and interest deducted from any payments made previous. The following items were reserved, viz: organ, bell, clock (belonging to the city), chandelier, pulpit and its furniture, and the corner-stone. [On examining this stone subsequently, its contents, to the disappointment of all, were found entirely moldered to dust. They had not been securely inclosed.] Before the sale, the society ordered that certificates be issued to the owners of pews for the amount of the recorded valuation of their pews, which should be received in payment for pews in the new church.

Concurrent with the foregoing sale, the trustees purchased a site for a new church on the southwest corner of Eighth and Elm streets, 145 feet on Elm and 150 on Eighth. In this purchase, the time and attention of the trustees were severely taxed, through November and December, 1871. The south part of the tract, 80 feet on Elm, was purchased of James T. Worthington, for $36,000 cash. The other part, 65 feet on Elm, was purchased of the heirs of Samuel Wiggins, for $35,000 cash. This part the trustees had arranged to secure on a perpetual lease, but this arrangement finally failed. This ground is part of the premises of Judge Burnet's family mansion, and the precise site of the proposed church was Mrs. Burnet's flower garden, in which she so much delighted. Here the trustees are proceeding to erect an edifice, which is expected to be both convenient and ornamental. In the meantime the society worship in the hall of the Cincinnati College.